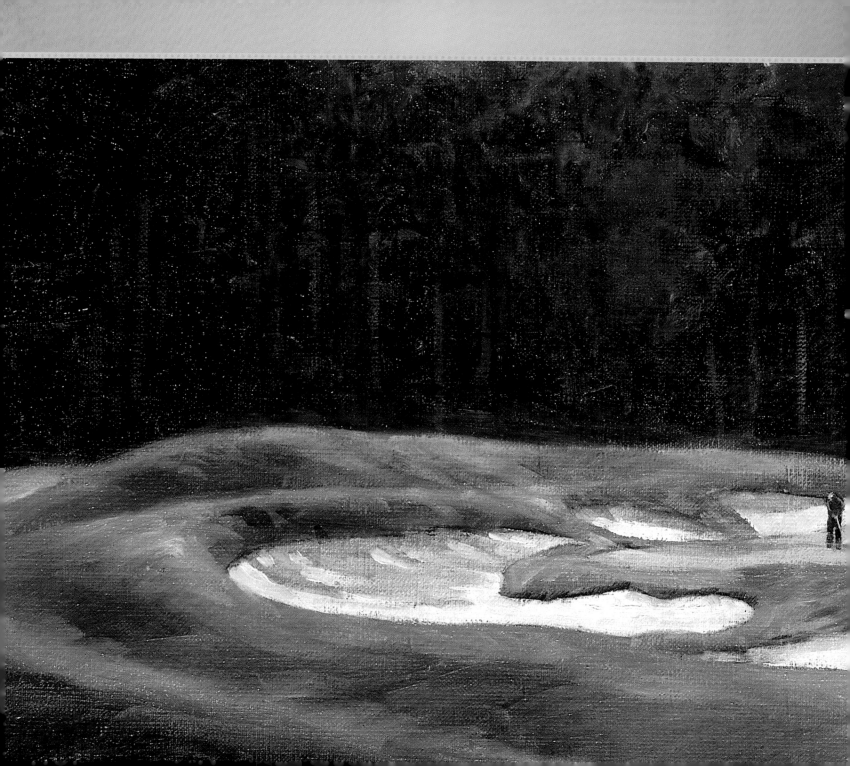

WHERE THE GRASS IS ALWAYS GREENER

Insight and Inspiration from the Fairway

Paintings by
DONNY FINLEY
Text compiled by Terry Glaspey

Harvest House Publishers
EUGENE, OREGON

Where the Grass Is Always Greener
Text Copyright © 2000 by Harvest House Publishers
Eugene, Oregon 97402

Library of Congress Cataloging-in-Publication Data

Finley, Donny.
    Where the grass is always greener /paintings by Donny Finley; text compiled by
Terry Glaspey.
        p.cm.
    ISBN 0-7369-0304-6
    1. Golf 2. Golf–Pictorial works. 3. Golf–Quotations, maxims, etc. I. Glaspey, Terry.
II. Title.

GV967.5 .F56 2000
796.352–dc21

00-027813

Artwork designs are reproduced under license from ©Arts Uniq'®, Inc., Cookeville, TN
and may not be reproduced without permission. For information regarding art prints
featured in this book, please contact:

    Arts Uniq'
    P.O. Box 3085
    Cookeville, TN 38502
    800-223-5020

Design and production by Koechel Peterson & Associates, Minneapolis, Minnesota

Terry Glaspey and Harvest House Publishers have made every effort to trace the
ownership of all poems and quotes. In the event of a question arising from the use of
a poem or a quote, we regret any error made and will be pleased to make the necessary
corrections in future editions of the book.

"On Target" is from *Just Like Jesus*, Max Lucado, 1998, Word Publishing, Nashville,
Tennessee. All rights reserved. Used by permission.

Scripture quotations are from the King James Version of the Bible.

Printed in Hong Kong.

01 02 03 04 05 06 07 08 09 / IM / 10 9 8 7 6 5 4 3 2

Donny Finley wishes to thank . . .

I would like to express my appreciation to Ted Higgins of Mount
Juliet Golf Club, who was instrumental in making contacts with
golf courses around Ireland, and to Dwight Carlisle, who has
been my driver, map reader, golfing partner, patron, and, most
of all, a good friend.

I would also like to thank the following golf courses for their
cooperation in making this book possible:

> Ballybunion Golf Club, County Kerry, Ireland
>
> County Sligo Golf Club, Rosses Point, County Sligo, Ireland
>
> Druid's Glen Golf Club, County Wicklow, Ireland
>
> Killarney Golf and Fishing Club, County Kerry, Ireland
>
> Lahinch Golf Club, Country Claire, Ireland
>
> Mount Juliet Golf Club, County Kilkenny, Ireland
>
> Old Head Golf Links, County Cork, Ireland
>
> Ring of Kerry Golf Club, County Kerry, Ireland
>
> Royal County Down Golf Club, County Down, Ireland
>
> Royal Portrash Golf Club, County Antrim, Ireland

A special thanks should go to my home course of Greystone
Golf Club, Birmingham, Alabama.

CONTENTS

Oh, golf is for smellin' heather and cut grass and walkin' fast across the countryside and feelin' the wind and watchin' the sun go down and seein' yer friends hit good shots and hittin' some yerself. It's love and it's feelin' the splendor of this good world.

—MICHAEL MURPHY
Golf in the Kingdom

THE CALL OF THE FAIRWAYS

Terry Glaspey

As you walk down the fairway of life, you must stop and smell the roses, for you only get to play one round.

—BEN HOGAN

To me, the ground here is hallowed. The grass grows greener, the trees bloom better, there is even warmth to the rocks. Somehow or other the sun seems to shine brighter on "The Country Club" than any other place I have known.

—FRANCIS OUIMET
ON THE BROOKLINE COUNTRY
CLUB (MASSACHUSETTS)

Golf courses are the answer to the world's problems. When I get out on that green carpet called a fairway and manage to poke the ball right down the middle, my surroundings look like a touch of heaven on earth.

—JIMMY DEMARET

On a spring morning, I climb out of bed before the sun has even begun to peek over the edge of the dark sky and I drive a handful of miles to a local public golf course. As the day begins to brighten, a dense morning fog settles in. I hit a few balls on the range before my tee time, watching most of them drift to the right before they disappear, enveloped in the fog. I can't tell how far they are going, but I can tell that they aren't going straight. Making a few adjustments to my stance, they begin to straighten out. It is nearly time to tee off so despite the density of the stubborn fog, I amble out to the first tee.

My first shot is a wild slice, which goes right at a sharp angle and comes to rest in the bushes along the fairway. "A good time for a mulligan," I mutter to myself, trying to come up with an excuse that could lay the blame on the fog, rather than on my rather questionable ability with the driver. Taking a deep breath, I adjust my stance and relax my grip a little. The next shot is a beauty, rising slowly from the tee box with the grace of bird taking flight. It is straight and long, at least by my hacker's standards. I smile as it reaches the apex of its climb skyward then disappears into the fog.

It is the kind of shot that keeps me coming back to this seemingly impossible-to-master sport. It is poetry in motion, as graceful as the movements of a ballet dancer. And the authoritative click of a well-struck ball on the clubface or the gentle plop as it drops to the green from the fairway are sounds as perfectly wonderful as any musical instrument can manage.

By the third hole, the sun has burned away the fog, revealing the course in all its splendor. The trees are filled with leaves and birdsong, the sun is breaking through them in shafts of shimmering light, and the green grass is mottled with patches of brightness. Squirrels chatter and frolic around the base of the trees, accompanied by the gentle gurgle of a small stream that meanders along the left side of the fairway. Dew glistens on the moist grass and my putts, when struck, trail a little spray of water behind them. The tracks the ball leaves mark its journey as it winds toward the cup. Everything seems fresh and newborn this morning. And I am glad to be here. There is a deep peace and gratefulness in my heart. Whether today's round is made up of birdies or triple bogies doesn't really matter all that much. This is simply a wonderful place to be.

Certainly it is the beauty of the golf course that is part of the lure of the game. The best courses combine the carefully manicured look of a park with the wildness of the outdoors. On any given great golf hole, the glory of God's creation is wedded to the ingenuity of man. As Robert Trent Jones, one of the greatest golf course designers ever, once said, "Golf courses are built by men, but God provides the venue."

Indeed He does. Here, amid the trees and green and the bunkers and the beauty, it is easier to let our mind be filled with the things that really matter. To find a moment of peace or self-awareness in the midst of our all-too-chaotic lives. If we open our eyes to the glory around us, a round of golf is not only great entertainment—it is also food for the soul.

No other game combines the wonder of nature with the discipline of sport in such carefully planned ways. A great golf course both frees and challenges a golfer's mind.

—TOM WATSON

What other people may find in poetry or art museums, I find in the flight of a good drive.

—ARNOLD PALMER

Even if you aren't having an extra good day, always count your blessings. Be thankful you are able to be out on a beautiful course. Most people in the world don't have that opportunity.

—FRED COUPLES

Don't hurry. Don't worry. You're only here for a short visit. So don't forget to stop and smell the roses.

—WALTER HAGEN

What a beautiful place a golf course is. From the meanest country pasture to the Pebble Beaches and St. Andrews of the world, a golf course is to me a holy ground. I feel God in the trees and grass and flowers, in the rabbits and the birds and the squirrels, in the sky and the water. I feel I am at home.

—HARVEY PENICK

THE CHARACTER OF THE GAME

You can spend a lot of money trying to learn about yourself.

Perhaps you've considered attending various kinds of seminars, seeing a psychologist, or undergoing testing that will help get to the bottom of who you are and what makes you tick. But any golfer can tell you that an easier way to come to some sort of self-understanding is to take up the game of golf. Golf has an unfailing ability to uncover our deepest personality flaws or bring to light our most desirable traits and virtues. Whether for good or bad, golf is the great revealer of character.

Golf is a game of blows and weapons. In order that the game continue, we must make amends for every single act of destruction. In a golf club everyone knows the player who does not replace his divot. One can guess how he leads the rest of his life.

— MICHAEL MURPHY

The only way of really finding out a man's true character is to play golf with him. In no other walk of life does the cloven hoof so quickly display itself.

— P. G. WODEHOUSE

Golf tells you much about character. Play a round of golf with someone, and you know them more intimately than you might from years of dinner parties.

— HARVEY PENICK

Golf may not teach character, but it reveals it.

— THOMAS BOSWELL

Golf brings out your assets and liabilities as a person.

— HALE IRWIN

Golf puts a man's character on the anvil and his richest qualities—patience, poise, and restraint—to the flame.

— BILLY CASPER

Golf is the infallible test...The man who can go into a patch of rough alone, with the knowledge that only God is watching him, and play his ball where it lies is the man who will serve you faithfully and well.

— P. G. WODEHOUSE

There is no other game which teaches honesty to the same extent as golf. There is no referee, and the rules are based on the assumption that every golfer is strictly honest. What other game depends on the integrity of the player to such an extent, that even if he is out in the rough, alone with his Maker, and loses a stroke because his ball rolls over in addressing it, he must at once acquaint his opponent with the penalty?

—ALISTER MacKENZIE

My Best Round Ever

Phil Callaway

For a mere two hundred and seventy dollars, you can golf all year round on the course near our small town. Not that you'd want to. In December it's colder than a polar bear's kiss here, and by January the only people on the first hole are ice fishermen who sit around fires shivering and dreaming of August. But for three months of summer, there's nothing finer than an early morning walk down our narrow fairways, avoiding creeks teeming with catfish, and tame deer who have been known to stroll over and check your scorecard.

I've golfed the finest courses in America, from Oregon's coast to Georgia's humidity, but none quite measure up to this nine-hole marvel near home.

Here I learned to golf.

And I've learned a few things about life, too.

When I was a boy my father told me to treat my friends as I would my golf clubs. "Take them out often, Son," he said, "and never let them beat you." I wasn't sure what he meant at the time (I was only three), but in the past few years I've come to discover that golf is a team sport. It's best enjoyed with a few good friends.

Of course, not all my friends love to golf. Dan Johnson, for instance, once told me that golf is "cow pasture pool" and a poor excuse for a sport. "Football—now there's a sport," said Dan, thumping his chest. "The only way you can get hurt playing golf is to get struck by lightning."

I took Dan golfing one stormy day and on the par three sixth hole, after he had lost every single white ball in my bag, he was struck—not by lightning—but by the fact that he was wrong. Sometimes golf *can* hurt you.

When we reached the green—a wonderfully nasty green which slopes like a ski hill and can only be reached by transversing two magnetic creeks—Dan kept on walking down the cart path, past the clubhouse and out to the parking lot, where he kicked small stones around until I arrived.

"Golf is a four letter word," he said through his teeth.

"I think I'll play six holes every time I come," I told him as we drove home in relative silence. "I shot 25 today—my best score yet."

Dan wasn't finding humor in much of anything. "Golf's no sport," he insisted. "It's an expensive way of playing marbles."

———— ✳ ————

Thankfully, not all my friends feel this way. Gord Robideau is an avid golfer in the sense that if he had to choose between playing a round and insuring world peace, he would want to know how many holes. Gord is a school teacher. For him golf is science, art, and physics all rolled into one class. When we play together, the competition is high. On the first hole, Gord stretches at length before teeing off. Then he tosses tufts of grass in the air, holds a wet finger to the wind, and talks to the ball: "Alright, little buddy," he says, "let's you and me be friends today. I'll swing...you say 'wonderful.'"

"You know," I tell Gord as we saunter toward the first sand trap, "in the time it takes you to hit the ball I could memorize *War and Peace* in the original Russian."

He laughs. But by the time the 18th hole has devoured our Top Flites and we've compared scores, I am the one who is laughing. I'm the winner by two strokes. Gord and I have an agreement: If he beats me, I buy him lunch. If I beat him, he accuses me of cheating.

"You have a special hole in your pocket," he says as we sip Coke. "You lost a ball in the rough on number seven so you released a replacement ball down your pant leg. I saw you."

"It's okay, Gord," I tell him. "I know how it feels. I lost once. At checkers."

"You know, Phil," he says, "you always manage to beat me somehow. But you've never beaten this course."

"What do you mean?"

"You've never parred it."

"Can't be done," I say. "Too much water...fairways slope to the creek...it's uphill even when it's downhill."

"Tell you what," says Gord with a wide grin. "You par this course and I'll buy you lunch for life...I'll pay your membership next year and throw in some mutual funds."

"Serious?"

"Well, I'm serious about lunch."

Now, please understand that I am a bogey golfer. I am also a cheapskate. So all that winter I practiced in our basement thinking about that free lunch. I strung up a net, carpeted a putting green, and memorized Arnold Palmer videos. By June, my swing was a mess. By July, the course had me beat. And by August, I'd salted away my clubs.

Then came the phone call. It was Dan Johnson. "Let's go golfing," he said.

"You okay, Dan?" I asked. "Did they switch your medication?"

"Naw...I'd...well...I'd just like to get away for a few hours. I need someone to talk to."

Dan drove the cart that day. And he told me of his marriage. Of his life. The mistakes behind him. The changes ahead. Sometimes he pulled out a club, but mostly he talked. I golfed. And listened. On the sixth hole we sat in the grass of the tee box, talking about golf and life. "The thing I love about golf," I told him, "is that each day is a fresh start. That's how it is with grace too. In our lives. In our marriages. We won't get perfect scores, but grace gives us hope."

Standing up, I pulled a six-iron from my bag and hit the straightest shot of my life, 162 yards over two greedy creeks. It landed two feet from the pin, spun backwards, momentarily clung to the lip of the cup and came to rest an inch from the hole. Dan watched in amazement.

"What's your score so far?" he asked.

"I haven't a clue," I said. "I don't dare think about it."

All day long I didn't miss a shot. I sunk three 15-foot putts, my pitching wedge made beautiful music, my driver delivered laser beams. As we sipped pop at the end of our round, Dan tallied my score and gasped in amazement. I was two under. Grabbing a cell phone, I called Gord.

"Ha, not a chance," he said.

"I have a witness," I said. "Lunch in an hour?"

"Okay, lunch in an hour."

It's been two years since that prime rib meal and the round of my life. I haven't even come close to par since. But I've been thinking about it. And realizing that no matter what the score, the best rounds of our lives come along when we're thinking of others, celebrating friendship, and talking about grace.

———

The only time my prayers are never answered is on the golf course.

— BILLY GRAHAM

Golf is 20 percent mechanics and technique. The other 80 percent is philosophy, humor, tragedy, romance, melodrama, companionship, camaraderie, cussedness, and conversation.

—GRANTLAND RICE

PRACTICE, PRACTICE, PRACTICE

Terry Glaspey

Golfers tend to have a mania for picking up new tips on how to improve their game. The inherent complexity of golf and the ever-present hope for improvement lead us on a constant quest for a better game. We search everywhere for help. We subscribe to all the best golf magazines, watch golf videos and the pros on TV, invest in all kinds of odd-looking training devices, and scour all the latest golf instruction books in search of the elusive tip that will take away our slice, make our drives go longer and straighter, or help us sink a higher percentage of those knee-knocking four foot putts. It is the hope for improvement that keeps us playing this wonderful and infuriating game.

The first step to improvement, whether it be our short game or our personal character, is to admit that we have a problem, something that needs fixing. The important thing is to remain teachable, always excited about the opportunity to learn something new, not to rest on our previous accomplishments. We should try to cultivate the attitude that we can always get better, that there is always something more we can learn. And then we need expose ourselves to those who can help us make strides toward our goal.

The wise and the prudent know that golf is like everything else in life: We stand to learn much from the experts, from those who have studied and experienced more than we have. We do not need to reinvent the best way to play the game. The same basic guidelines for a good swing have stood the test of time, from Bobby Jones to Ben Hogan to Jack Nicklaus to Tiger Woods. The equipment has vastly improved over time, but the fundamentals of the game itself remain the same. Therefore, we can learn a lot from the masters, from those who have excelled at this sport.

*Learn from the skillful.
He who teaches himself hath a fool
for his master.*

— BEN FRANKLIN

*Golf tips are like aspirin.
One may do you good, but if you
swallow the whole bottle, you will
be lucky to survive.*

— HARVEY PENICK

*Don't be too proud
to take lessons. I'm not.*

— JACK NICKLAUS

*You must work very hard to
become a natural golfer.*

— GARY PLAYER

The constant undying hope for improvement makes golf so exquisitely worth playing.

—BERNARD DARWIN

Preparation through steady practice is the only honest avenue to achieving your potential.

— CHI CHI RODRIGUEZ

The harder you work, the luckier you get.

— GARY PLAYER

Every day you miss playing or practicing is one day longer it takes to be good.

— BEN HOGAN

Correct one fault at a time. Concentrate on the one fault you want to overcome.

— SAM SNEAD

Focus on remedies, not faults.

— JACK NICKLAUS

If we only rely on what we can learn from ourselves, we will never get very far. Very few great golfers are self-taught. In golf, as in life, we need to draw on the wisdom of others.

But memorizing tips and learning theories is not enough. We may be able to visualize what a great swing looks like, able to diagram each step of the takeaway, the turn, the impact, and the finish. We may understand what such a swing looks like, but until we can actually do it ourselves, it will not improve our score by a single stroke. This "head knowledge" will not actually make us any better as a golfer. To really improve requires effort. It requires the forming of good habits.

All athletes must commit themselves to extensive practice if they want to excel at their chosen sport. The ability to smash a home run out beyond center field, to consistently sink baskets from behind the three-point line, to throw a 50-yard pass that arrives with pinpoint accuracy, to stroke a golf ball 150 yards to within a few feet of the pin—none of these abilities comes automatically. Sure, any of us might be able to perform one of these feats on occasion, but to do so with the kind of regularity that the professional athlete manages, requires commitment to practice. Skill comes through practice. In any area of our life, whether it be an aspect of our golf game or a personality flaw we want to overcome, we must practice doing it right until it becomes second nature, an ingrained habit. As one pro golfer said with a glint in his eye after chipping the ball into the cup from well off the putting surface: "It's amazing how lucky you get when you practice this several hours a day!"

When the great player makes a mistake he says, "I'm going to work on that and not do it again." The bad player says, "Boy, I messed up again. I guess I really am a dog."

— PETER JACOBSEN

THE ESSENCE OF THE GAME

Bob Welch

I return to golf courses to play golf for the same reason, I suppose, that my late father returned to rivers to fish: to catch the one that got away. Somewhere out there, I'm convinced, is this 275-yard drive that will rise like an F-15 from the deck of an aircraft carrier, hang in the sky for what seems like minutes, then split the fairway with the precision of my mother cutting a peanut-butter sandwich cleanly in half when I was a boy. Somewhere out there is an approach shot that heads for the pin like a heat-seeking missile. Somewhere out there is a triple-breaking, downhill putt that I have never made but am utterly convinced I will.

Meanwhile, back at the reality ranch, I might duck-hook a drive into a blackberry thicket, nail my brother-in-law in the back with an approach shot (as I did not long ago), and three-putt from 20 feet.

Lives there a sport that is more delicious and diabolical than golf?

I have spent my life immersed in sports, having played games, watched them, officiated them, and written about them for newspapers and magazines such as *Sports Illustrated* and *Runner's World*. But golf holds a grip on me in a way that the others do not.

Just as it is a complex game to play, so is it a complex game to understand. But not long ago, because of a slow group in front of our foursome, I found myself with 10 minutes to simply sit on a fairway mound and contemplate the meaning of golf. I was 210 yards away on a dogleg-left par-5—water left of the green. Since I rarely have an opportunity to get home in two on such a hole, I was anxious to see if I could hit a 5-wood on the green and make birdie. And yet the moment was so quiet, so perfect, that I felt the unexpected pleasure of simply immersing myself in it.

We were playing a hillside gem called Diamond Woods in the heart of Oregon's Willamette Valley, a lush track carved through what once had been a Christmas tree farm. It was late October, a weekday afternoon. The sun would soon slip behind the Coast Range, not only for the day, I sensed, but perhaps for months while Oregon went into its winter hibernation of clouds and drizzle.

This, then, is part of the allure of golf, the aesthetics you don't find in, say, a bowling alley: the sheer beauty of a golf course. Moulded by man, yes, but created by God: water and grass and trees and contour. Shade and slope and sun and light. And, of course, color—an array of color. An hour west of here, a mile from the crashing Pacific Ocean, you walk up the seventh fairway of Sand Pines Golf Course and, in one view, can see horizontal layers of color: the blue of the sky, the green of Douglas fir forests, the white of sand dunes, the rich green of the fairways—all sandwiched together like Neapolitan ice cream.

Here at Diamond Woods on this October afternoon, the course is framed in fall: oak and maple in their subtle oranges and yellows. The ponds are blue and so still that they beg you to pull out a rock and see if you can skip it clear across. A creek meanders through the woods; now shallow and spent by a dry summer, it will, by Christmas, be swift and cold.

It all begs you to connect not only with what my wife's grandmother loved to call "God's handiwork," but with one's self. We live in a noisy, fast-paced world. What simple joy to walk toward one's drive and simply feel free to think.

In a sense, you could say golf is an escape. But you could also say that it's an escape toward the profound: rest, relaxation, God's beauty, and people we care about. When the guy on the adjacent fairway is getting ready to hit and his cell phone rings—perhaps that's the sound of a ball and chain, the world hounding us to return to the trivial.

As I survey this autumn scene, I see another reason that golf has a hold on me: my 20-year-old son Ryan, home from college on a break, stands behind his drive on the other side of the fairway, 10 yards closer to the green than me.

I am one of those people who has enjoyed playing golf by myself; as a boy, I would, on uncrowded days, play two balls and pit Arnie (Palmer) vs. Jack (Nicklaus). But I also love the way golf lends itself to relationships. To small talk. To occasional big talk. And, of course, to the proverbial banter of guys whose talk is usually more impressive than their swings.

When Ryan was 15, we awoke one August morning

just before dawn in my grandfather's beach cabin. We drove seven miles north, walked onto the beach and sunk a soup can in the sand, then put a branch with a seaweed "flag" in it. We then drove back to the cabin, took out our drivers and, just as the sun hinted its arrival, teed off on our creation: a 7-mile long golf hole.

It was a par-72, we decided, and, ironically, we both shot four-under-par 68s. But the real value of the endeavor had nothing to do with balls and clubs and scores, and everything to do with fathers and sons. With a relationship.

It is hard to relate with someone when you're trying to cut them off on the baseline or tackle them or throw them out at first base. But golf offers the opportunity for people to connect.

Golf, in that sense, is a gentleman's sport. A player's competitive fires can be burning deep inside and yet the interaction between two golfers can be completely civil. To be sure, exceptions exist; but more than other sports, golf seems to breed a certain spirit of cooperation between players. We help each other look for a lost ball. We give each other yardages. We tend the pin for one another.

What's more, golf breeds a sense of honor in that players police themselves. Again, I'm not naive enough to believe all golfers live up to that code, but most do. Once, in a round of golf in which we were both playing poorly enough that cutting a few strokes here and there wouldn't have been noticed by the other guy, my brother-in-law hacked around in the trees, finally found the green, rolled in a putt and announced he'd had a 14. I've seen professional golfers call two-stroke penalties on themselves

simply because their ball moved as they addressed it with their club. Honor is important and golf helps breed it.

As I awaited my shot on this October afternoon, I realized the daylight was going fast; with 10 holes to play, we would probably play the final few holes in near darkness and might even wish we had one of those airport ground-crew guys with their flashlights to guide us home the final few holes. This, too, is the appeal of golf: it's ever changing. The course looks different now than it will look an hour from now.

In April, I would not be going for this green in two. In April, my drive would have plugged 30 yards back and I would be laying up with a five-iron and playing safe for par. Golf is governed by ever-changing elements.

Weather, of course, is one of them. Earlier this year, I played an Oregon beachside course, Bandon Dunes, that golf magazines are saying is the rival of Pebble Beach. Having played both, I agree. But a 30 mph wind meant sometimes hitting a four-iron in situations where I'd normally hit a nine-iron. It was British Open golf with a Southern twist: my score was gone with the wind.

Golf courses are never the same twice. A 15-foot putt in the dewy morning will be slower and break less than that same putt in the afternoon. On this day, the tees were up, the pin left-center; tomorrow, on this same hole, the tees may be back and the pin right-front.

But I digress. The foursome ahead of us has putted out. It is time, finally, for The Shot. My two friends and son watch as I take my stance and prepare to swing. The

On the golf course, a man may be the dogged victim of inexorable fate, be struck down by an appalling stroke of tragedy, become the hero of unbelievable melodrama, or the clown in a side-splitting comedy— any of these within a few hours, and all without having to bury a corpse or repair a tangled personality.

— B O B B Y   J O N E S

They say golf is like life but don't believe them. Golf is more complicated than that.

— G A R D N E R   D I C K I N S O N

Golf is so popular simply because it is the best game in the world at which to be bad. At golf it is the bad player who gets the most strokes.

— A. A.   M I L N E

flag, back-left on a kidney-shaped green, teases me. Draw the ball even slightly and my Titleist will find a watery grave. Miss the green right and I'll be hitting over a series of camel-back mounds.

This is what golf does so well: tests you, dares you, challenges you. On a shot like this, it doesn't matter whether I'm Tiger Woods or the 18-handicapper that I am. I have a sense of opportunity, of possibility, of potential. The beauty of the moment is so perfect—the scenery, the weather, the playing partners and, of course, the opportunity. I feel as if anything but a perfect shot will spoil it all, like falling when water-skiing on glass-smooth water.

The time has come. I swing hard and like the feel of the contact. I have struck the ball well. Alas, my water worries apparently have sent the subliminal message to my body to keep the ball right. It flies right of the green, bounces hard on a mound and kicks into an adjacent fairway—pin high, but 40 yards away.

There is nothing better than seeing a well-struck shot go where you intended it. But as I walk to the ball, I sense little dejection. For the golf experience is so much more than a single shot, or even the sum total of all those shots that culminate with two or three numbers: 69, 83, 98, 119....

The golf experience is the sound of a Canada goose in the distance as you stand over a putt and the way your son's arm punches the sky when he sinks a birdie, and the camaraderie between your foursome as you wait to hit. The score—the numbers—isn't the fullest expression of the experience; it lies much deeper, in what you'll remember about the day when you're hibernating in that Oregon winter.

Besides, before I loft a wedge over the mounds and make a pretty decent two-putt for par, I have already decided something during this late-season round: I'll be back. As my father would say, you have to go after the one that got away.

Thus, do we return to the river. Thus, do we return to the course.

A SCHOOL FOR HUMILITY

Terry Glaspey

My friend stood on the first tee and waggled his driver, trying to loosen the tension in his arms and legs and contemplating his first shot.

Bottom line was this: He wanted to make an impression.

He was golfing for the first time with a couple of new clients. He stood to benefit greatly from the camaraderie that often develops during a round of golf, so he'd invited them to play a round at one of the nicer courses in town. This particular account had proven very difficult to land and it had not been easy to break the ice, but the suggestion of playing a round of golf together had done the trick—they were very enthusiastic about the idea. Then he learned that they were pretty serious golfers, not just the once-a-month variety. Once they began talking about it, it became obvious that they were far better golfers than he was. He joked with them about the fact that they'd probably beat him soundly, but they laughed with that sort of knowing laugh which indicated they thought it was just gamesmanship on his part. "All right", my friend said to himself, "I'll just have to get my game into shape." So he had played each day for the past two weeks to get himself prepared for today's outing and to fend off the embarrassment of making them endure 18 holes of bad golfing on his part.

He stepped up and assessed his shot. If he could get his opening drive out past the 240 yard markers, it would take the trees to the right out of play and open up the green for his second shot. He knew from experience that this shot was within his ability, but he also knew that he'd have to give it a pretty healthy whack to get there. He waggled a couple of times, took the club back in a fluid motion, and swung down and through with all his might.

Despite his efforts, two unfortunate things happened.

Golf is the hardest game in the world. There's no way you can ever get it. Just when you think you do, the game jumps up and puts you in your place.
—BEN CRENSHAW

Golf is a game of getting used to failure.
—DAVID DUVAL

Golf is the humbling game and none know that better than the best.
—THOMAS BOSWELL

Do your best, one shot at a time, and then move on. Remember that golf is just a game.
—NANCY LOPEZ

First, he completely missed the ball, passing over it with just enough velocity for it to tip gently off the tee.

Second, he had swung with such might that the follow-through continued, sending him into a twirling, balletic pirouette, then with tangled feet, depositing him in a collapsed heap on the grass. He lay there, unhurt but for his pride, wishing there was a sandtrap somewhere nearby that he could bury himself in. Looking up from the freshly mown grass, he saw his golfing partners trying to pretend they hadn't witnessed his mortifying little maneuver, and struggling mightily to keep a straight face.

Yes, he had definitely made an impression. It just wasn't quite the one he'd intended.

Golf can be a humbling game. No matter how well we think we have mastered this sport, we will soon be reminded that, just like in life, we must learn the extent of our own limitations. Though a risky over-confident shot will sometimes be rewarded with a marvelous outcome, more often it will land us in trouble. And usually while others are looking.

No one is immune from the humility lessons that golf will sometimes dispense. Humans are not born with a natural ability to steer a small white ball four hundred yards and into a hole the size of a drinking cup. We work hard to develop this skill, and in spite of all that effort, the skill sometimes deserts us. The game of golf reminds us that no one is capable of perfection all the time. Have we not all, on occasion, seen even the greatest golfers in the world hit shots that were downright embarrassing—whiffs, shanks, duck hooks, putts that broke the opposite of the way they were read, or gallery-threatening misfires?

In a very real way, golf gives us an important insight into the nature of pride. We all seek and strive to impress others with our gifts, our talents, and our abilities. But we are all imperfect, flawed, capable of much less than we might want to think. In life, as in golf, we will pay a price for the conceit of thinking more highly of ourselves than we ought. Sometimes a badly hit 7-iron is a more powerful reminder than any sermon on the evils of overweening pride.

Golf is assuredly a mystifying game. It would seem that if a person has hit a golf ball correctly a thousand times, he should be able to duplicate the performance at will. But this is certainly not the case.

— BOBBY JONES

Golf is an open exhibition of overwhelming ambition, courage deflated by stupidity, skill soured by a whiff of arrogance. These humiliations are the essence of golf.

—ALISTAIR COOKE

Success in golf depends less on strength of body than upon strength of mind and character.

—ARNOLD PALMER

IT'S A FUNNY GAME...

Golf has always had to deal with detractors, with those who consider the game to be elitist, a boring waste of time, or a foolish pursuit for a grown-up adult. The mania and passion of the golfer have made them the target of all kinds of good-natured--and some not-so-good-natured--criticism down through the years. The golfer tends to take it good-naturedly and laughs at such criticisms, realizing that there may well be a grain of truth in there somewhere. But usually, he is more occupied with thinking about his next round...

Golf increases the blood pressure, ruins the disposition, spoils the digestion, induces neurasthenia, hurts the eyes, calluses the hands, ties kinks in the nervous system, debauches the morals, drives men to drink or homicide, breaks up the family, turns the ductless glands into internal warts, corrodes the pneumogastric nerve, breaks off the edges of the vertebrae, induces spinal meningitis and progressive mendacity, and starts angina pectoris.

— DR. A. S. LAMB (CIRCA 1900)

The hardest shot is a mashie at ninety yards from the green, where the ball has to be played against an oak tree, bounces back into a sand trap, hits a stone, bounces on the green, and then rolls into the cup. That shot is so difficult I have only made it once.

— ZEPPO MARX

Golf is a lot of walking...broken up by disappointment and bad arithmetic.

— ANONYMOUS

Golf is an ineffectual attempt to direct an uncontrollable sphere into an inaccessible hole with instruments ill-adapted to the purpose.

— WINSTON CHURCHILL

One of the advantages bowling has over golf is that you seldom lose a bowling ball.

— DON CARTER, PROFESSIONAL BOWLER

Golf lacks something for me. It would be better if once in a while someone came up from behind and tackled you just as you were hitting the ball.

— HAROLD "RED" GRANGE

A WINDOW OF WONDER

Steve Overman

"A good walk spoiled" was Mark Twain's famous characterization of the game of golf. H. L. Mencken thought that anyone "found guilty of golf" should be appropriately censured. And while the game was still relatively new, a 1457 decree by King James outlawed its practice, due to what he considered its deleterious effects (especially on the Scottish military). Even today, golf still has its detractors. When you consider the rising cost of the game, the amount of time it takes to complete a round, and the gargantuan effort required to master this elusive game, one can't help but wonder if they have a point. Maybe golf is an unfit pursuit for a responsible adult...

What then, is it that beguiles so many growing millions all over the world not only to indulge in, but passionately pursue, the repeated beating and chasing of a little white ball?

My first tastes of golf were as a caddy. It was as a bag carrier for club members that, in an almost sacred stillness, I first smelled the fresh dew on Indian Hills Country Club's fairways and first witnessed the poetic trajectory of a well-struck shot. It was also as a caddy that I experienced some of the wildness that Bill Murray made famous and funny in his movie, *Caddyshack*. There at Indian Hills this suburban kid first rubbed shoulders with young men from Chicago's inner city. I learned to play poker and sensed the sting of cold, caddyshack justice when my friend Tom was ceremoniously "ponded" for allegedly cheating at cards.

I can recall many long summer days when, absent a Little League game, my friends and I would finish our "loops" at Indian Hills and ride our bikes to the public course where $35 bought us playing privileges for the whole summer, excluding early mornings and weekends. Sometimes I played with my fellow thirteen-year-old golfing buddy, Dave Missantoni, or with a couple other friends. Other times I went golfing by myself, in bare feet, playing a couple of balls, until early evening would become the dark of night and finally force a finish to a full day.

Through the years, golf has been a friend. What is it that makes this game so uniquely special?

I've loved the experience of camaraderie a game of golf can create. I've loved the deep, rich solitude that seems so poignant when you're alone on the course, but which is somehow still present even in the company

of fellow adventurers. I love the rhythm within each round and space you can find within which to dream, to commune, and to renew. So little else in life seems to provide this experience.

In golf, the natural elements are also part of the experience. The sun, the wind, and the rain, the temperature and humidity, even the varied regional topographies, flora, and grasses, all conspire to make each round an encounter with a new creation.

Then there is the sense of integrity the game tends to create. In how many other modern games do the competitors police themselves, in fact derive great honor from calling penalties on themselves that no one else could possibly have detected—even penalties that may seem unfair or even contrary to the spirit underlying the rule in question? This is, of course, part of the rich ethos of golf—where tradition matters and honor is universally upheld as a matter of personal pride. To me, the private nature of this obedience makes it especially powerful.

It is true that golf is a very difficult, sometimes torturous, game. But for golfers like me, this too is a feather in its cap. Those with a tendency to be obsessive-compulsive love the fact that golf is infinitely detailed and difficult to master. As I journey deeper into the game I am always discovering yet another set of factors that affect the success of a shot. This process of unfolding seems unending.

Golf reminds me of some important truths about life. Golf, like life, can be unfair. Of course I love it when I am the recipient of an incredibly lucky bounce (although I suppose I usually try to downplay it, as though my originally errant shot were not really that bad!). But I've even come to grudgingly appreciate the fact that it is possible to play a relatively accurate shot and have the bounce go the other way as well. That's just the nature of the game!

With a young family and a growing set of other responsibilities, these days a round of golf doesn't "fit" as often as it used to. But when it does, somehow this strange game, developed and evolved over centuries, continues to provide for me "a window of wonder."

Donny Finley

A Few Unusual

"LOCAL RULES"

FROM AROUND THE WORLD

NYANZA G.C. IN BRITISH EAST AFRICA, 1950:
If a ball comes to rest in dangerous proximity
to a hippopotamus or crocodile, another
ball may be dropped at a safe distance, no
nearer the hole, without penalty.

A RHODESIAN GOLF COURSE, 1972:
A stroke may be played again if interrupted
by gunfire or sudden explosion.

JINGA G.C. IN UGANDA:
On the green, a ball lying in a hippo
footmark may be lifted and placed not nearer
the hole without penalty.

BJORKLIDEN ARCTIC G.C. IN SWEDEN:
If a reindeer eats your ball, drop another
where the incident occurred.

ON TARGET

Max Lucado

The golf game was tied with four holes to go. As we stood on the tee box, I spotted the next green. "Sure seems like a long way off," I commented. No one spoke. "Sure is a narrow fairway," I said as I teed up my ball. Again, no response. "How do they expect us to hit over those trees?" Still no answer.

The silence didn't disturb me. Years of ruthless competition against fellow ministers on municipal courses has taught me to be wary of their tricks. I knew exactly what they were doing. Intimidated by my impressive streak of bogeys, they resolved to psych me out (after all, we were playing for a soda). So I stepped up to the ball and took a swing. There is no other way to describe what happened next—*I hit a great drive.* A high arching fade over the crop of trees to my left. I could hear the other guys groan. I assumed they were jealous. After watching their drives, I knew they were. None of them even made it close to the trees. Rather than hit left, they each hit right and ended up miles from the green. That's when I should have suspected something, but I didn't.

They walked down their side of the fairway, and I walked down mine. But rather than find my ball sitting up on thick fairway grass, I discovered it hidden in weeds and rocks and surrounded by trees. "This is a tough hole," I muttered to myself. Nevertheless, I was up for the challenge. I studied the shot and selected a strategy, took out a club, and—forgive me but I must say it again—*I hit a great shot.* You would have thought my ball was radar controlled: narrowly missing one branch, sweeping around another, heading toward the green like a jackrabbit dashing for supper. Only the steep hill kept it from rolling onto the putting surface.

I'd learned from televised tournaments how to act in such moments. I froze my follow-through just long enough for the photographers to take their pictures, then I gave my club a twirl. With one hand I waved to the crowd, with the other I handed my club to my caddie. Of course, in my case there was no photographer or caddie, and there was no crowd. Not even my buddies were watching. They were all on the other side of the fairway, looking in the other direction. A bit miffed that my skill had gone unnoticed, I shouldered my clubs and started walking to the green.

Again, it should have occurred to me that something was wrong. The tally of curious events should've gotten my attention. No one commenting on the difficulty of the hole. No one complimenting my drive. Everyone else hitting to the right while I hit to the left. A perfect drive landing in the rough. My splendid approach shot, unseen. It should have occurred to me, but it didn't. Only as I neared the green did anything seem unusual. Some players were already putting! Players whom I'd never seen before. Players who, I assumed, were either horribly slow or lost. I looked around for my group only to find them also on the green—on a *different* green.

That's when it hit me. I'd played the wrong hole! I had picked out the wrong target. I had thought we were playing to the green on the left when we were supposed to play to the green on the right! All of a sudden everything made sense. My buddies hit to the right because they were supposed to. The groan I heard after my drive was one of pity, not admiration. No wonder the hole seemed hard—I was playing in the wrong direction. How discouraging. Golf is tough enough as it is. It's even tougher when you're headed the wrong way.

The same can be said about life. Life is tough enough as it is. It's even tougher when we're headed in the wrong direction.

One of the incredible abilities of Jesus was to stay on target. His life never got off track. Not once do we find him walking down the wrong side of the fairway. He had no money, no computers, no jets, no administrative assistants or staff; yet Jesus did what many of us fail to do. He kept his life on course.

As Jesus looked across the horizon of his future, he could see many targets. Many flags were flapping in the wind, each of which he could have pursued. He could have been a political revolutionary. He could have been a national leader. He could have been content to be a teacher and educate minds or to be a physician and heal bodies. But in the end he chose to be a Savior and save souls.

Golf is a game of endless predicaments.

—CHI CHI RODRIGUEZ

PAR FOR THE COURSE

Terry Glaspey

One of the worst mistakes you can make in golf is trying to force the game.

— JACK NICKLAUS

Every day on the golf course is about making little adjustments, taking what you've got on that day and finding the way to deal with it.

— TIGER WOODS

As I get older, I try to think of the bad things that happen to me on the golf course as "tests." They're not hurdles; they're not bad marks or punishments. They're things I need in my life, things that bring me back to reality.

— FRANK BEARD

Golf isn't fair. It doesn't take very many rounds before this truth impresses itself upon you. How many times has your perfectly struck shot headed straight for its target, only to hit a small mound and go careening off into trouble? How many times has just an inch meant the difference between landing in the water and staying safely perched on the edge of the green? How often has a putt needed just one more rotation to drop gently into the cup, but instead run out of steam--and left you steaming? Such a small margin...

Of course it sometimes works the other way around. We sometimes get much better than we deserve. Standing on the seventeenth tee at a nearby course, on a tee box atop a hill that overlooks the fairway, I took my aim and sliced a terrible drive into a grove of trees. The ball should probably have struck a tree and fallen into the pine straw, where I'd be lucky to get it back onto the fairway with my next shot. Instead, it bounced around in the midst of the trees and bounded back into the very center of the fairway, in a superb position for my shot to the green.

No golf isn't fair. But then again, neither is life.

The mature golfer, just like any other mature person, knows that the "slings and arrows of outrageous fortune" are a part of life. We must be prepared to deal with whatever comes next, whether it be what we had hoped for or whether it be that which we most fear. In life, as in golf, we must be patient. We must take the good with the bad, trusting that things usually have a way of evening themselves out.

Without the cavernous bunkers and the ravenous water hazards, without the bad breaks and the good ones, golf would surely lose much of its interest. Overcoming the challenges is part of its appeal. In the same way, learning to be patient and meeting the challenge of overcoming our struggles is what molds us into people of character, people who know how to be graceful in the face of whatever life may throw at us. Just as golf must be played one shot at a time, so our lives must be lived one day at a time—with patience and the sense of hope that there will always be another day.

One of the things that is so wonderful about golf is that you always have a second chance.

I was about 80 yards from the green and had a pretty decent lie in the light rough on a short par four. I took a couple of practice swings to get the feel for how hard to hit the shot and consciously tried to relax. Sometimes I'll tense up over a pitch shot and chunk it or send it sailing over the green. Not this time. I made clean contact with the ball and sent it in a perfect arch toward the pin. It landed short, hopped once, and then rolled straight toward the hole, turned left just at the end and rattled into the cup. But not, as you might suppose, for an eagle. This miraculous shot was for *par*. I'd duck-hooked my drive into the deep rough, chopped out with an ill-hit 7-iron, and then sent a topped 9-iron skittering across the grass to the point from which I could take my fourth shot. It wasn't pretty, but it was a par—just the same as if I'd hit two good shots to the green and two-putted.

This is one of the things I love about golf. In a certain sense, every shot lets you start all over again. Sure, the last shot may have left you in a bit of a predicament, but you always have a fresh opportunity to right your mistake. And if you manage to make a muddle of an entire hole, ballooning to a triple bogey or worse, there is always a fresh hole just ahead to help you redeem your dignity.

There is, in this, a parable we can hold onto as we live our lives: It is never too late for a new beginning. Surely the most amazing promise in the entire Bible is contained in these words: "If any man be in Christ, he is a new creature: old things are passed away; behold, all things are become new" (2 Corinthians 5:17). That is the hope of the gospel, God's good news. No matter what a mess we might have made of our lives, God can give us a new start. We can begin anew. Every day. Unlike a golf score, our previous "bad scores" do not remain part of our history. They are forgiven and forgotten. God tears up the old score card and offers us the chance to begin the round again. All we need to do is ask.

And as we make our way through the course of our life, trying to avoid the hazards and discover the deepest truths about ourselves, there is no better playing partner than our Creator. He gives us the hope that comes from a second chance and the courage to keep trying. His love guides and strengthens us for what lies ahead. We glimpse His glory and we know we are loved.

Like life, golf is a game of good breaks and bad breaks.
There is nothing fair about it.
— HARVEY PENICK

The game isn't fair, but then life isn't fair either.
— LEE TREVINO

❦

No one can succeed at golf until he has mastered the art of not permitting one bad hole, or indeed one bad shot, to affect the rest of his game.
— HENRY LONGHURST

❦

Don't be afraid to be patient.
— CURTIS STRANGE

❦

We must all play the ball as we find it.
— BOBBY JONES

❦

Don't consider losses a waste of time. Consider them an apprenticeship.
— GREG NORMAN

❦

Take your lies as they come. Take the bad bounces with the good ones.
— BEN CRENSHAW

I can sum it up like this:
Thank God
for the game of golf.

— A RNOLD P ALMER